LUCID DREAMING

THE BEST LUCID DREAMING TECHNIQUES AND TIPS FOR OBE AND LUCID DREAMING

ANGEL MENDEZ

CONTENTS

Introduction   v
Presentation   ix

Chapter 1	1
Chapter 2	7
Chapter 3	12
Chapter 4	17
Chapter 5	19
Chapter 6	27
Chapter 7	30
Chapter 8	33
Chapter 9	37
Chapter 10	39
Chapter 11	40
Conclusion	43
Sneak Peek - Chapter 1	49

©Copyright 2022 by Angel Mendez
All rights Reserved

ISBN: 978-1-63970-146-9

In no way is it legal to reproduce, duplicate, or transmit any part of this document in either electronic means or in printed format. Recording of this publication is strictly prohibited and any storage of this document is not allowed unless with written permission from the publisher. All rights are reserved.
Respective authors own all copyrights not held by the publisher.

❦ Created with Vellum

INTRODUCTION

This book contains proven steps and strategies on how to manage practical life situations and challenges.

Taking the time to practice the method of Lucid dream meditation will help with your subconscious mind issues and will keep them from getting blocked up with any traumas you may be experiencing in this lifetime and even some that you may have brought with you from a previous lifetime.

Lucid dreaming brings about more stupendous sensitivity toward oneself and self-esteem, encouraging a genuine and consistent natural immunizing process. Opening to all the more light inside our being with conscious dreams likewise opens our awareness to consciousness association and alignment with well-being and Cosmos Love.

A lucid dream is a fantasy in which you know you are dreaming. Sometimes this happens when the visionary experiences something abnormal, and when they stop to question their circumstances, they understand they are in a fantasy.

Lucid dreams happen naturally, albeit some individuals may have them commonly more often than others. The meaning of lucid dreaming may be basic; however, there are considerable measures of misguided predictions for it.

The meaning of lucid dreaming may be simple, and there are great deals of misinterpretations surrounding it.

Lucid dreaming is your opportunity to play around with the phenomenal capabilities covered in hidden parts of your mind. Notwithstanding whether you are superhuman in genuine or not, lucid dreaming is a path for you to put the deepest zones of your mind to great use while you're sleeping.

Dreams are created during a time of deep sleep which is termed REM. Everybody dreams every night; however, sometimes then they don't remember anything they envisioned.

Due to this, some people accept they don't dream at all. However, this is not the situation. We need to remember our dreams, and inevitably we could remember two or three of the dreams, perhaps more.

After getting up in the morning, relax and make an effort not to move around much. Permitting your body to relax helps keep your mind in a sleeping mode for some moments. This helps you recollect your dreams better.

Abstain from sitting in front of the TV or being on the computer work for an hour before bed. The splendid lights can make it harder for sound sleep, hinder your inner sleeping process, and damage your capacity to review dreams.

Taking vitamin B6 supplements has been demonstrated to enhance remembering capacity.

Drinking a glass of apple juice a few hours before going to sleep can help, while sustenance, such as fish, bananas, chicken, and turkey, are great sources of vitamin B6 that you can try if you would prefer not to take the vitamin pills.

Chocolate has likewise been beneficial for work, despite not being as adequately in a few cases. Find out what lives up to expectations for you and stick with it!

Let yourself believe that you will recall your dreams. Rehashing "I will remember my dreams in the morning" or something like yourself will cause set up your mind to review what you envisioned in the night and serve as a kind of positive impact.

The mind is very effective, and on lucid envisioning, there isn't any hindrance in bringing it to its maximum capacity.

Have certainty that you will remember your dreams! Conviction is a paramount part of lucid dreaming, for review and in addition controlling your dreams.

You could be a Supreme for the moment and superman while sleeping. All the manifestations of reality might be put aside; as you make the experience the inner part of the mind or test your craziest science probes your most exceedingly terrible adversaries.

PRESENTATION

Lucid dreaming is mindfulness that you are imagining. This mindfulness can go from an extremely swoon distinction of reality to something as manifestation as the growth of awareness past what has ever been accomplished, even in waking life.

Lucid dreams naturally happen while an individual is amidst a consistent dream and suddenly aware that they are dreaming. When you understand this, you will control your dreams, which is essentially the most basic part of lucid dreaming.

CHAPTER 1

What does "LUCID DREAM" mean?

Despite the fact that the expression "lucid" means clear, lucid dreaming is more than simply having a normal dream. To have a lucid dream, you must realize that it's a fantasy while you're dreaming. That is it.

It doesn't oblige that you can control anything in your dream, however, control is the thing that starting lucid visionaries frequently go for. Individuals get pulled into lucid dreaming on the grounds that they need to have the capacity to do things they could never do in waking reality, for instance, fly to the sky.

More accomplished lucid visionaries understand the benefits of clear imagining. You can utilize it to investigate the limits of your mind and the unlimited parts of the universe.

. . .

What's the best process for getting to be lucid in dreams?

The best process for getting to be LUCD is to be more aware and look and listen and give careful consideration to points of interest, as when you see things that don't fit, that is an intimation that you're imagining.

To encourage the process, you can structure the propensity of analyzing nature's domain or your state of awareness amid the day. For example, mental propensities you work on amid the day have a tendency to proceed in dreams.

So you analyze your surroundings amid the day, you look at your mindfulness, and afterward, you may perceive that something is diverse once you begin imagining. Somebody who has gotten to be clear has much larger amounts of mindfulness, and clearly, Ii is found that is one of the greatest benefits of lucid dreaming.

A Dream isn't clear unless you control it!

There is some disarray about the distinction in the middle of clarity and dream control. The two are connected; however, one can happen without the other. Still, some of the lucid dreams experience almost no control in a few instances. Then again, it is conceivable to practice some fantasy control without being mindful that it is a fantasy. Normally the fantasy plot will clarify this by making the visionary accept divine control over everything. Dream control, by our definition, could be either conscious or oblivious.

. . .

Lucid dreaming is New Age

Since we all have clear dreams commonly now and then, we realize that any one perspective does not constrain clear envisioning.

There are verifiable records which discuss clear imagining doing a reversal a large number of years- -so it is scarcely another sensation. There is no compelling reason to have any profound convictions to revel in clear dreams.

Clear imagining Supporters' Idealism

Lucid dreaming happens while you are sleeping; it is not implied at all to infringe upon your inclusion in this present reality. While numerous clear visionaries appreciate recording their fantasies, discussing their fantasies, and arranging fun clear dreams, this is, for the most part, the same as another distraction.

Truth be told, playing a feature amusement or viewing a motion picture will take you out of "this present reality" more than clear envisioning will.

Clear imagining is unique & includes Mysterious

Numerous religious or spiritual groups' are protuberance of clear imagining in with mysterious practices and exercises. On the other hand, transparent dreams regularly happen commonly, and there is nothing mysterious about them.

Numerous extraordinary religious epiphanies and messages came as dreams; in some cases, clear dreams. Our dreams are what we make them; whether we wish to provide for them profound centrality or not is dependent upon us.

Dreams contain messages that are lost with Lucid Dreaming

As of this composition, there are numerous speculations concerning why dreams exist and what reason they serve, but none of these hypotheses have been demonstrated so far.

One hypothesis is that our fantasies contain important or helpful messages about our lives. Considering that numerous individuals don't significantly recall their fantasies without considering changing the fantasy plot in a small amount's one had always wanted is in examination not almost as risky for any message-sending done through dreams.

Lucid dreaming requires great dream review regardless of the possibility that a small amount of these messages are lost in clear dreams.

You are likely recollecting a lot of more normal dreams than you ever did some time recently, and on top of that, providing for them more consideration than at any other time.

Levels of Lucidity & Dream Control

. . .

Clear imagining was characterized as getting to be mindful.

The genuine level of mindfulness shifts, on the other hand. When clarity is high, you are well mindful that nothing you encounter is true, and you understand that you don't have anything to fear. You can't be hurt by any circumstances that may appear unstable.

With low-level clarity, even though somewhat mindful you are imagining, you are not mindful enough to have an incredible effect on your dream. You may accept a few parts of your dreams that you would not naturally accept in the routine.

With low-level clarity, your acknowledgment might additionally rapidly blur, and you may acknowledge the entire dream as reality.

A lucid dream is a regular and sound experience. It is much like another dream aside from the little distinction of your information that it is a fantasy. It has nothing to do with the new age, the mysterious, or idealism, nor would it be able to damage you any more than a consistent dream could.

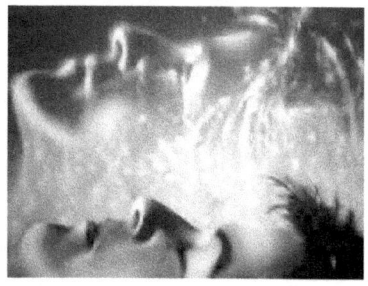

Keep a dream journal close by your cot during the evening, and compose in it quickly in the wake of waking. On the other hand, you can keep a recording gadget off chance that you think it is simpler to rehash your fantasy so everyone can hear.

This helps you perceive your regular dream components (individuals from your past, particular spots, and so on.), furthermore tells your mind that you are not kidding about recalling your fantasies!

It will additionally help you to perceive things that are one of a kind to your fantasies. You will have the capacity to perceive your own "fantasy signs." These will be repeating things or occasions that you may recognize in your fantasies.

By being mindful of your slumber plan, you can organize your example to help actuate clear dreams.

Concentrates on determinedly recommend that a snooze a couple of hours in the morning wake is the most widely recognized time to have a clear dream.

Lucid dreams are unequivocally connected with REM rest. REM sleep is condensed just before the last wakening. This implies they most usually happen just before waking up.

CHAPTER 2

Astral Projection

Astral projection helps a state of profound relaxation, so it ought to be performed in a place of your home where you're comfortable. Lie on your couch and relax your mind and body.

It's simpler to perform astral projection alone than it is with another person in the room. So if you comfortably rest with an accomplice, pick a room other than the room to practice astral projection.

Draw the shades or draperies and free the room of hindering commotions. Any kind of interference could upset the state of relaxation you have to attain.

Position yourself on your back in your picked room. Shut your eyes and try to clear your mind of diverting thinking processes.

Focus on your body and how it feels. The objective is to accomplish a state of complete mind and body relaxation.

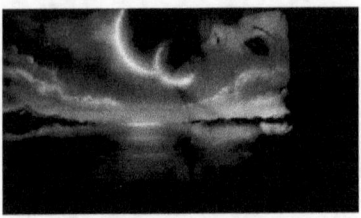

Flex your muscles and then slacken them. Begin with your toes and work your path up to your body, step by step going to your head. Be sure that each muscle is loose when you are through.

Inhale profoundly and breathe out totally. Don't hold pressure in your chest and shoulders. Simply relax.

Center your mind on your relaxing. Don't escape with thoughts of outside stresses, and don't get distracted with the thought of your soul anticipating from your body. Instead, simply let yourself sink into relaxation.

This entrancing state is typically known as the hypnogogic state. Let your body and mind method rest, yet don't lose consciousness. Being at the edge of awareness and sleep, a mesmerizing state is essential for astral projection to happen
Achieve this state using the below-mentioned technique:
Keeping your eyes closed, let your mind meander to a part of your body, for instance, your hand, foot, or a solitary toe.

. . .

Concentrate on the body part until you can envision it impeccably, even with your eyes closed. Then, keep concentrating until all different thoughts fall away.

Use your brain to flex your body part. However, don't physically move it. For example, envision your toes twisting and uncurling or your fingers holding and unclenching until it appears to be as if they are physically moving.

Grow your awareness to other parts of your body. Move your legs, your arms, and your head using just your mind. Keep your center relentless until you're ready to move your entire body in your mind alone.

Some people report feeling vibrations, which come in waves at various frequencies, as the soul gets ready to leave the body. Don't be perplexed about the vibrations since the vicinity of alarm may make you leave your meditative state; rather, succumb to the vibrations as your soul gets ready to leave your body.

Envision in your mind the room in which you are lying. Move your body in your brain to remain up. Look around yourself. Get up off the informal lodging over the room, then turn around and take a gander at your body on the couch.

Your awareness is effective if you feel as if you are looking upon your body from over the room and that your conscious self is now separate from your body.

. . .

It takes a considerable time of practice to get to this point. If you experience difficulty-totally lifting your soul from your body, take a stab at lifting simply a hand or a leg right away. Then, continue rehearsing until you're equipped to move over the room.

Your soul dependably stays united with your body with undetectable energy once in a while, alluded to as a Silver Rope. Let the power manage your soul again to your body. Reemerge your body. Move your fingers and toes physically, not just in your mind, and let yourself recapture full awareness.

When you have aced the demonstration of anticipating your soul from your body in the same room, you will need to affirm that you were indeed in two different planes.

Next time you practice astral projection, don't turn around to take a gander at your body. Instead, leave the room and stroll into another room of your home.

Look at an item in the other room, something that you had never recognized previously in the physical sense. Make a mental note of its shade, shape, and size, carefully considering whatever a number of subtle elements could be allowed.

Come back to your body. Physically go into the room you beforehand anticipated yourself into. Stroll to the article you analyzed during the astral travel.

. . .

Will you affirm the points of interest you noted when you investigated the item with your mind?

During consequent astral projection sessions, go to areas that are unique to you. Each one time, note subtle elements that you had never perceived previously. After every session, physically confirm the points of interest.

After a couple of outings, you will be accomplished enough to go to areas that are new to the trust that you have really performed astral projection.

Some say that astral projection is unsafe, particularly when one gets enough practice to investigate new places. However, it is pleasant to envision yourself showered in a shining- Silver White Light before your astral undertaking.

Envision it as a sky around you; this will secure you from other thinking processes. However, there is such a great amount to get into. Realize that no damage will come to you unless you think it will. The rush of having an awareness keeps some individuals out of their bodies for long times of time, which is said to debilitate the silver line.

CHAPTER 3

Make sure to stay aware of your body while your soul is anticipated somewhere else.

The silver string can never be broken; however, it is said that your soul might be deferred from returning your body if you use a lot of vitality outside of it.

Some say that evil spirits can possess the body while the spirit is continuously anticipated. If you fear this may happen, ensure your body by gifting the room with a prayer to God before you perform projection.

Your spirit can also interface with other astral projections. Try it with a companion who has practiced to the extent that you have. Some say astral sex is mind-blowing. Be that as it may, remember to come back to your body naturally.

. . .

Essentially, it means that when you nod off, you convey your awareness from when you were astir simply into REM sleep and began as a lucid dream.

Try to contemplate into a quiet, however, centered state. You can have a go at numbering breaths, imaging rising or sliding stairs, dropping through the Cosmos, being in a calm soundproof zone, and so on.

A simple approach to get your body to the edge of sleep is by lying in your informal lodging your awareness onto the again of your head where it touches the pad (pillow).

Hold up until your inner voice stop. Then you can envision sinking into your cushion until your body is pretty much sleeping. Now move your awareness out of your body while trying to clutch your awareness as firmly as would be prudent. This will mean your body nods off, and you will pass clearly into the dream world.

Try to picture your life, alert and dream-life, as aspects on a precious stone when you practice. Some decide to call this jewel the Supreme, others God, and even your soul. The point here is to start to perceive what life is experiencing at the same time.

It is just our "Recognition" that orchestrates our shows into direct or "timed" prayer. As exactly as a jewel may be, every feature, if seen as an individual experience, is still happening in the meantime the "Dream Body" experiences. Remember that it is simply a slight movement in mindfulness that this activity calls for.

Each time you recognize the during your waking hours challenge whether you are astir or sleeping. In the end, you may see them in your sleep and get to be clear.

Make at least three natural awakenings each time something appears to be unheard of, emphatically disappointing, or irrational, and that propensity will bear on into your lucid dream.

These will let you know that you are resting in a lucid dream, permitting you to relax up clear. To recollect doing natural awakenings in dreams, you have to propensity to do awakenings in genuine living.

One natural awakening approach is to search for "dream signs" (components that regularly happen during your dreams, find out for these in your diary), or things that would not ordinarily exist in normal living, and then lead the natural awakenings.

When these activities become a propensity, individuals will start to release their dreams and reach the conclusion they envision.

Often doing natural awakenings can balance out dreams. A few strategies incorporate Looking at a clock to check whether it stays consistent, looking at a collection of content, turning away, and after that thinking over to check whether it has changed.

. . .

Looking in a meditative state (your picture will frequently seem blurry or not show up at all in a dream) while your figure could be horrendously distorted in a mirror, fearing you into a bad dream or a fantasy.

Looking at your hands and asking yourself, "am I envisioning?" (When imagining, you will frequently see more noteworthy or less than five fingers on your hand).

Hopping circulating everywhere; you are naturally ready to fly amid dreams Jabbing yourself; when envisioning, your body parts may be more versatile than in normal living; a typical rude awakening is pushing your finger through the palm of your hand.

Remind yourself even as you turn or fall that you imagine, as you will end up in a diverse area when you quit turning or hit the ground and may lose clarity normally.

If you feel a fantasy "shakes" or is going to become dull, look down to the ground and picture your surroundings, reminding yourself you are envisioning.

If you begin to perceive themes in your fantasies, you will recognize dream signs or certain things that keep on reappearing in your dreams. This may be as basic as all fantasies are in your patio, or everything you could ever hope for has fans in them.

. . .

Get into the propensity of doing dream checks each time you see your fantasy sign, and in the end, you'll see your fantasy sign in a lucid dream, do a check and understand you're envisioning.

Simple Techniques & Tips for Lucid Dreaming
Use at least 20 minutes of time in the daytime to practice a lucid dream. The techniques to use here incorporate meditation, self suggestions, and visualization of what you desire to include in your plans.

Meditation is innovative of the subconscious mind. When you practice meditating profoundly, you can experience some captivating phenomena, including mental illusions, feelings of bliss, and sudden inner experiences.

Meditation harmonizes you into your waking reality on upper levels and helps you feel more settled in your routine life.

Research has interfaced meditation with simple, lucid dreaming for many reasons. Initially, it prepares you to enter higher states of mindfulness.

Second, it harmonizes the link between your conscious and subconscious mind. Thirdly it makes you more aware, helping you to perceive the illusion of the dream world and get to be clear all the more naturally.

Begin by practicing a basic 20 minutes morning meditation into your daily routine, for instance, a simple breathing practice.

CHAPTER 4

Morning Exercise- Mild Breathing Technique

First phase (10 Minutes):
You have to sit by keeping a distance to confirm that disciples who might want to lie down may do this effortlessly.

. . .

Nobody will talk; gone will be the chattering whatsoever. Instead, every one of you will take a seat quietly.

Shut your eyes and begin breathing profoundly. Inhale to the extent that you can, and additionally breathe out to the extent that you can.

Put your entire energy in breathing in and breathing out basically, inhale profoundly and breathe out profoundly.

Apply yourself completely and work indefatigably together using the deep breathing process for the first ten minutes.

Permit every fiber of the body to vibrate together utilizing breathing in and breathing out, and also be aware that you're breathing in & out profoundly. Continue observing in which air is going out and coming in continuously.

Observe from inside that breathing is coming in and going out on a general premise, consistently and in addition energetically.

Deep shake of breathing will start to arouse some vitality inside you. Together along with utilizing your fiery breathing in and breathing out, a dormant light in you will shine up.

CHAPTER 5

Second Phase (10 Minutes):
Now you must forget your body completely and relax. First, take a deep breath and after that, leave your body free. For 10 minutes, keep breathing deeply.

At the moments of relaxation- Make an inner suggestion, "I will enter and observe my dreams with awareness."

If the body takes specific postures and likewise motions – permit it to take them. Simultaneously don't ease off your breathing.

Whatsoever happens in your body empowers it completely; don't come in its path whatsoever. Don't withhold anything.

The vitality is arousing, so breathe in and breathe out essentially and after that leave the body uninhibited and free.

. . .

Let go of the body and don't dither for the incoming feelings. Let them come and wash away.

The more you apply efforts, the more rest will be accessible. The higher the development you raise, the deeper the vitality will go down in you.

Let whatever happens to the body happen it openly.

Now drop all exertions of breathing practice and enter the last phase of relaxation.

Give up everything and for 10 minutes lie in observing for the flash of the inner mind happenings/functioning of the thoughts.

At the moments of relaxation- Make an inner suggestion, "I will enter and observe my dreams with awareness."

Now open your eyes gradually and further inhale profoundly, however gradually, and then get up tenderly.

Its merry being anything completely, as once your total being is indulged; the sums of the inert energies of the body collect together and collaborate with you.

. . .

If you lurch through your waking life in a haze, make it a propensity to take more observation of the outer world. Some individuals use a great deal of their day with an inner centering.

If you continually give careful consideration to the sights, sounds, and shades of the world, you'll improve the probability of spotting something out of your dream world.

Music can trigger pretty much any feeling you can consider. Play a CD or run your iPod through a set of speaker's bedside your couch as you sleep.

Find out some music that triggers strong memories or feelings and blend those tracks with relaxing mood melodies. Then, make a playlist and let it circle as you stay asleep all night.

Taking nourishments with healthy flavors (spices) has an intriguing impact on the body, exactly as taking a few medications can work.

These can trigger irregular or striking dreams, both of which are a decent thing in case you're figuring out how to have a lucid dream and attempting to remember and control your dreams.

For lucid visionaries, the apprehension or concern is that the distinction of a dream may bring about the visionary awakening.

. . .

It's conceivable that "awakening" is false when it truly demonstrates a loss of control over the dream as the subconscious mind assumes control.

Get into the propensity of doing with awareness each time you wake up, and you can control this from happening.

Before you go to sleep at night, rehash this to yourself: "I will remember perceiving that I'm envisioning." Remembering this in your mind with awareness will intuitively convey into your dreams.

Realize that in your dream, you will recall that you are dreaming. Therefore, it is essential part to have lucid dreams.

Try to recognize your dream signs. The best and most essential method for deciding your dream signs is by keeping a dream diary.

At whatever point you check it, you can undoubtedly recognize those dream signs that are regularly happening. Then, at the moment when your future dreams contain them, you will understand it's simply a dream sign.

Envision yourself being again to a past dream. However, this time, you need to re-live the consummation unexpectedly.

Picture the scene in the fantasy in such a path to the point that the points of interest are clearer than what is reachable in the past dream.

Next, try to desire the dream signs! Obviously, this ought to be some unique characters, areas, and circumstances that ought to uncover a negligible dream, something you wouldn't see in genuine living.

Next, begin letting yourself know what you are envisioning. Then, in spite of the fact that you are dreaming (and this is in no way, shape, or form a clear dream), keep on experiencing an envisioned lucid dream.

Do whatever you would do if this were a genuine clear dream.

Research has demonstrated that awakening sleep can expand one's possibility of being lucid. In this way, to have more clear dreams, you may need to wake yourself up in the night and bring yourself to full consciousness for a few moments.

You can use those few minutes in perusing lucid dreams, meditating, picturing, and so on. Then, possibly set a clock/mobile alarm at 3 or 4 am.

On occasion, you may wake up amidst the night and end up in this dreamy state. If this happens, there is no requirement for you to freeze for your body and mind are relaxed.

Simply float into the dream world, and naturally, this can undoubtedly be finished without the slightest exertion.

This step includes venturing into the clear world, and this implies submerging your mindfulness completely into the clear dream and settling the fantasy to release any possibility of awakening.

Stay calm, don't get over-energized, and wake yourself up. Understand that you are envisioning, and keep your thoughts gathered right now inner your lucid dream.

Have some good times! It's an eminent experience to have, and there is nothing anybody or anything can do in a clear dream to damage you.

. . .

In the event that you end up frightened, when you get to be clear, realize that you are continually being guided and ensured and that you can wake yourself up whenever you wish.

It's imperative to recollect that there is nothing to fear in a lucid dream. A few people you experience may alarm you; however, remember all that you experience is an impression of yourself.

Cherish them and excuse them, and realize that you adore and pardon a part of you when you do so.

Diligence is additionally a paramount piece of figuring out how to lucid dream. Not everybody will attain accomplishment with the same methods or at the same time. It's essential to perceive that fantasy is typically a discussion with your subconscious mind.

To know how to clear dreams is to see how to be tuned in to yourself. That implies giving careful consideration to things in your waking life that you ordinarily don't.

Perhaps the most energizing (and frequently scary) part of clear imagining is the capability to adjust the fantasy itself. Since you are mindful of the dreams that you know aren't genuine and are just the result of your brain, you can take control of the fantasy itself.

Dream control is moderately basic and rests on one thing - desires. Accepting emphatically and as completely as you can that something will happen or work a certain way is the best strategy for dream control.

To a certain degree, they likewise depend on visualization. For example, if you anticipate that somebody will turn around the bend and walk towards you, don't simply indiscriminately summon them and let the fantasy do the rest.

If you don't imagine what they look like, which gets to be simple with practice, the dream will fill in the missing subtle elements, and the individual may look off, or something about them may not look right.

This goes the same for changing areas and other dream control practices.

CHAPTER 6

What are the Spiritual Benefits of Lucid Dreams?

That being said, it unquestionably makes you a more illuminated individual. You figure out how to be right now and to perceive your surroundings, and take in things without being diverted from arbitrary musings or the past or what's to come.

That is the thing that all spiritual experts show you now: The significance of being right now. Those are the things that lucid dreaming has been doing the whole time. They are aware and mindful of the present moment with their physical body, as their body is stretched to incorporate a higher self.

Have there been any studies endeavoring to measure identity changes previously, then after the fact lucid dreaming?

. . .

Of course! Some individuals have taken a gander at the attributes of lucid dreams. For example, one study auditing a diary was about clear visionaries perceiving things in change sightlessness and mindfulness difficulty seeing standards quicker than normal individuals.

Clear visionaries are normally better at recognizing things in light of the increased mindfulness.

Could clear imagining be risky? For example, assume individuals erroneously think they are imagining and begin doing insane things.

No, it's not a potential issue for lucid dreaming. By definition, clear visionaries know they are imagining, so they are not confused about when they dream and are conscious.

In any case, non-clear visionaries could get confounded in the middle of imagining and being aware. Individuals simply beginning may need to take it simple and not stuff fire in their mouth or bounce out from a precipice to see what happens.

An accomplished, clear visionary would never bounce off a precipice without first testing whether they could skim buzzing around.

Does clear imagining ever make you tired? Do you ever feel like being clear in your dreams and not getting sufficient sleep?

. . .

There is some worth in non-clear dreams; however, those are the ones that are tiring. That is to say, who needs to be parting ways with a secondary school beau once more and be feeling all hopeless?

Who needs to take that test and stress over some test outcome when you're not even in school any longer?

It's the clear dreams that are reviving and fun. Clear dreams, not natural dreams, provide for me vitality and make me wake up feeling revived. You ought to try it!

CHAPTER 7

Concept of Lucid Dreaming

There are many benefits of lucid dreaming that are known where to begin when discussing them. The benefits of lucid dreaming start with having the capacity to develop stress easing through your dreams at any rate. That is the particular case that is proven.

Be that as it may, lucid dreaming can have numerous other health benefits throughout your life. Here are only a part of the benefits of lucid dreaming in the lives of many people:

Stress Relief

This is one of my most loved benefits of lucid envisioning. Amid especially unpleasant times, it's been a gigantic shelter to have the capacity to enter into a clear dream and take a relaxation. So many individuals use sex in clear dreams for anxiety alleviation, or they may carry on dreams where they're beating all the terrible fellows in their lives, speaking to busting all the anxiety elements they have right now.

Essential Thinking Skills

Many researchers and mathematicians see this as the best of the benefits of lucid envisioning. They can practice an issue in their fantasies. Moreover, since the mind is working alternately, it will naturally make new associations you wouldn't have considered, making it less demanding to think of approaches to care for issues.

Likewise, you can utilize clear dreams to take care of issues in your interpersonal life by going for different positive results and perceiving how they play out in your dream.

Innovativeness Boost

Many individuals are super inventive in their clear dreams, and you could be deliberately so. For example, a few painters and designers use lucid dreams to discover thoughts they use in genuine living, and artists can also create true music in dreams.

Regardless of the possibility that you aren't in an imaginative calling, it could be fascinating to perceive how your mind makes new associations on an intuitive level, and you can take some of this innovativeness with you into your commonplace life.

Practice Skills

In clear dreams, Psychologist Stephen states that you can practice physical aptitudes to enhance them about whether. Numerous technique specialists, pilots, and other individuals whose employments rely on their capacity to arrange particular activities productively hone their aptitudes in lucid dreams.

This is one of the unique benefits of lucid envisioning since it can set genuine associations in the cerebrum to make these activities more regular in ordinary life.

Confronting Fears
Some individuals use clear dreams to overcome fears of bad dreams. You can set up your clear dream to face the direst outcome imaginable, so you realize that you can traverse it.

You can also use your dreams to gradually experience your apprehensions and to know you can overcome them. It may also be used to combat unpleasant little things.

These aren't the main benefits profits of lucid dreaming, yet they're the ones that are normally getting notifications from other individuals and experiences.

The best way to experience all these benefits of lucid dreaming is to begin doing it! Look through whatever remains to get plans regarding how to begin lucid envisioning and to control your fantasies to experience your reasons for alarm, practice key abilities, or assuage anxiety accumulated in routine life.

CHAPTER 8

Enhanced Subconscious Mind

Lucid dreaming helps you prepare a significant part of the subconscious stirring in your mind that occupies you and keeps you from having the capacity to focus on a current workload.

When you calm these voices, your capability to think discriminatingly and tackle issues expands altogether. Researchers comprehend the benefits of lucid dreaming; some have used it to improve their essential thinking abilities in remarkably imaginative ways.

Take Friedrich Kerulen's revelation of the structure of the benzene particle, Otto Loewi's probe nerve motivations, and Elias Howe's development of the sewing machine. These dream-roused developments highlight the staggering force of the imagining intuitive personality.

. . .

When you take in the essentials of lucid dreaming, you can tackle issues on interest and a whole new level. That is on account you are not constrained by your legitimate conscious mind.

Rather, you can tackle issues imaginatively in nature's turf or by drawing deeper bits of knowledge specifically from your subconscious mind. Then, simply put any question to your lucid dream and be aware of the answer.

Mozart, Beethoven, and Wagner indicated dreams as the source of their inventiveness. Probably the loveliest music ever heard happens in lucid dreams. They invent our most imaginative side due to the free stream of plans emerging from the intuitive personality.

When you control your dreams, you can confront your apprehensions head-on and figure out how to overcome them. These triumphs will persist in your waking life and will enable you with another feeling of self-assurance.

Do you need trust in the waking scene? Assuming this is the case, you can use conscious dreaming, releasing your hindrances and completely free in a practical dream world.

If you need to enhance your open talking capabilities, you can practice the occasion in a lucid dream. Then, having honed your discourse on the earth, you will discover you have more trust regarding making the discourse in genuine living.

. . .

Keep in mind that careful discipline brings about promising results. Lucid dreams are a play area for experimentation. You can go for any idea comprehensible from business, games, and connections- anything you like.

By practicing a circumstance or essentially toying with distinctive conclusions, you can enhance your trust in any number of waking situations.

What are the profound established tensions that fill you with unease?

You can resist them in the safe environment of a lucid dream and comprehend what you have to do in your waking life to determine these issues and accomplish a more elevated amount of peace.

Do you experience the ill effects of concentration issues? Looking to lose weight, perhaps, losing weight is something that practically everyone might want to do eventually in their life, both for wellbeing reasons and for self-image.

It may be to quit unfortunate propensities and seek after a healthier lifestyle. When you control your dreams, you can enter into a spellbinding toward oneself state in which you can retrain your mind to receive healthier practices.

Hypnotic specialists perceive the estimation of dreams for uncovering data from the intuitive personality and venting blockages and disappointments as remedial change happens. They know the force of dynamic creative ability in trance and the waking state.

Think the amount all the more influential that dynamic creative energy could be in envisioning. Dream substance is as clear and rich as discernment amid the waking state actually, considerably all the more so.

The dream world is multi-dimensional, thus demonstrating that studies have indicated physiological reactions as though the occasion were really happening.

Nightmares are dreams where YOU are the victimized person. Anyhow when you control your fantasies, you are no more the victimized person. If you so pick, you can transform bad gloves into innocuous butterflies and pursue him away with a slugging stick.

Furthermore, if you have a repeating bad dream that has tormented you for quite some time, you can pick an alternate consummation for it. Lastly, practice the evening evil spirits that have been frightful for you for so long.

CHAPTER 9

Enhanced Memory

Do you ever wonder where all your overlooked memories go? They're still in your mind, and they're so profoundly covered your surface mind can no more get to them. But, be that as it may, when you clear dream, you can remember those memories and extraordinarily stretch your forces of review.

Sleep issues are regularly the consequence of lingering anxiety and tension. Yet when you figure out how to clear your dream, you can resolve the issues bringing about that push and uneasiness.

Not just that, when you use your nights having unbelievable encounters, for instance, flying, practicing mighty powers, shape-moving into whatever creature you need, you will be eager to go to rest every night on the grounds that you will be so eager to leave on your next nighttime escapade.

. . .

Apprehensions and bad dreams can pulverize individuals to the point that rest turns into a tormenting affiliation. You can confront these reasons for alarm and bad dreams with lucid dreaming, realizing that you are sheltered and can't be harmed.

Envision likewise can change instances of your dreams to help you win victory over those nightmares.

CHAPTER 10

Higher Vitality Levels

This one takes after naturally upon the keep going. If you are doing better around evening time, then you will be better rested amid the day. Also, when you've used the entire night battling off super villains, you will wake up feeling supercharged and prepared to undertake anything the waking scene will challenge you!

The benefits of lucid dreaming are extensive?
    Conscious envisioning permits you to face your apprehensions in a controlled setting. If you are perplexed about statures, why not bounce out of a plane?

You can ease off time for a controlled fall and buoy tenderly to the ground in the substitute reality of clear dreams. When you have done this at 10,000 feet, you will be amazed at how you feel about statures in the waking scene.

CHAPTER 11

Unravel Life Challenges

Natural thinking is without a doubt conceivable in cognizant envisioning. In a clear dream, you can dispose of traumas, fear, tensions, and various different issues; you can create new aptitudes, venture out to captivating places, et cetera.

Doubtlessly, conscious envisioning is the most ideal approach to guarantee that the intuitive piece of your psyche works for you.

You may accept that fantasies are the irregular sparkles created by concoction forms in the mind, or typical planets in which we consistently replay and reevaluate the experiences of our waking life, or portals to a multi-dimensional universe our weak human personalities can scarcely fathom.

. . .

Whatever your considerations on dreams, there's no denying that creating a stronger association with your subliminal personality can bring about colossal profits to your waking life — profits you would be insane to overlook.

CONCLUSION

How can it function? One clarification is that managing the direst outcome imaginable positively makes new neural examples in your subliminal personality.

Fortifying that conviction with more encounters that appear to be true can break up the apprehension by and large. From skydiving to bugs!

He may provide for you a surprising reaction that at long last permits you to support your trepidation) you can confront your reasons for alarm and reinvent your subconscious responses, realizing that truly no damage can come to you.

Envision for a brief moment that you had a gem that you could pose any question, and it would reply.

This gem could let you know anything you need to think about yourself.

Things you have bolted away inside. Some possibilities might be discharged, for instance, extraordinary memories and unique skills.

This gem exists when you clear dream. When you dream, you are in immediate contact with your subliminal personality.

However, this immediate access is a fortune and one of the profits of apparent imagining, just if one knows how to use it effectively.

Getting to be conscious of your dreams is the first step. Request what you need is the second. Ask, and you should get.

Do Anything You Want in Your Dreams, Naughty or Nice
We all have longing, dreams, and needs that go unfulfilled during our lives.

When you clear dream, all these wishes might be fulfilled, so you don't need to fixate on them. Instead, you can encounter whatever your deepest dream may be:

Discuss the significance of existence with Einstein.
Make love with a superstar.
Cruise the infinite seas on a spaceship.
Have a cookout amidst the earth.

Regardless of what your yearning is, you can satisfy it in your fantasies. When you have tasted this longing, it could be an incredible chance to see where that strong craving originates from in your being.

Shockingly Better, Blissful, and More Restful Sleep
Bringing more attention to your slumber and dreams provides for you a more soothing slumber.

Genuine unwinding happens when you can unwind while keeping up cognizance.

That is lucid dreaming and clear rest, basically.

We feel that we unwind when we sit before a TV; however, we are essentially taking in more incitement. Therefore, the psyche and body don't unwind in those circumstances.

The individuals who rehearse lucid dreaming practically discover they are more rested and have a greatly improved association with their slumber by and large. This is one of the top benefits of clear envisioning that individuals report.

Everybody cherishes a decent sleep.

Drastically Improve Your Memory
Your sleep is a source of cementing your memories of waking life.

Dreams set what is called verbose memory, while profound slumber cements semantic memory. Long-winded memory is similar to muscle memory, the memory of your body.

It is the memory you have to learn new aptitudes and impeccable the ones you have now. Semantic memory is fundamentally the capacity to recall truths. Think about a map book.

If you can recall each reality and figure from a map book, you have incredible semantic memory. Clear imagining and clear rest permit you to cement all you learned amid the day and deliberately pick what different things you need to set in your memory.

When understudies get some information about the benefits of clear envisioning, this is regularly at the highest point of their interest list.

Take in a Delightful Skill in One Night

All expert players long for their game amid the night.

Some people use visualization to enhance their diversion. Why?

Since they long for scoring an objective, the example of neuronal initiation in their mind is nearly identical as though they were scoring that objective.

That implies the best competitors train when they dream as well.

This entire world is interested in you amid cognizant envisioning.

You can choose to learn guitar, do a handstand, ride a cruiser, or another ability you may need to learn. You can destroy it a safe and the earth.

Lucid dreaming exhibits the way that the world we see is a build of our brains. It drives us to look past regular encounters and pose the question, "If this is not genuine, then what is it?"

The conscious dream is a fascinating background. The authenticity is astonishing.

It's against this foundation that you can confront your reasons for alarm, upgrade your inventive critical thinking abilities, enhance your certainty and practice new skills.

That is also the gigantic fun that originates from playing inside your reality dream world and how it identifies with your subconscious mind. Before long, you will see it is all interconnected, conscious, and oblivious, empowering you to use this play area for significant self-improvement and bits of knowledge.

Lucid dreaming is an expertise that anybody can create with inspiration and exertion. The satisfaction and profits are well worth the trouble.

What would you be able to do with the third of your life that is used to sleeping? How would you be able to utilize it to benefit the other two-thirds?

The line between the dream world and the waking scene starts to smudge through clarity, giving exceptional chances to communicate deliberately with your intuitive mind!

ACKNOWLEDGEMENT

I hope this book was able to help you to evolve your spiritual life. Lucid dreaming encourages an individual to go simply to their inner source of imagination to animate plans and tackle issues. Your subconscious mind is the source of inventive enthusiasm.

Numerous aesthetic experts Salvador Dali, William Blake, Paul Klee, Mozart, and Beethoven among them, say they thought of their best plans while sleeping.

By creating immediate, liberated access to your subconscious mind and then figuring out how to control it your ability for innovative speculation will result. Conscious dreaming is a naturally effective approach to enhance your inventiveness.

The next step is to practice as per the mentioned techniques of having Lucid Dreaming.
    THE END.

Did you like this book? Then you'll LOVE Lucid Dreaming: A

Guide to Lucid Dreams That Teaches You How to Lucid Dream and Control Dreams

This book contains proven steps and strategies on a lucid dream and becoming consciously aware of dreaming while in the dream state. Some people consider lucid or conscious dreaming a fascinating playground for the mind where you could fly over treetops, push through walls, make objects appear, even walk on water (inside your dream, that is), all while being conscious in the dream state. However, lucid dreams can open your mind to a world of infinite possibilities; lucid dreaming offers a gateway to so much more. This book is for those who have never experienced a lucid dream or do not truly understand that experience. Those who already have experienced lucid dreams will find different techniques, tips, and challenges to consider in their lucid explorations.

Lucid Dreaming: A Guide to Lucid Dreams That Teaches You How to Lucid Dream and Control Dreams

https://books2read.com/u/m2YJnd

SNEAK PEEK - CHAPTER 1

Lucid Dreaming: A Guide to Lucid Dreams That Teaches You How to Lucid Dream and Control Dreams

https://books2read.com/u/m2YJnd

What is Lucid Dreaming?

It's hard to wrap your head around the fact that such a mystifying and magical skill exists. It's even harder when you step back and realize that a great many of us in the past and the present go through our whole lives without even trying to master the art of lucid dreaming. Just think about it. Some of the best experiences in our lives happen in our dreams. How often have we exclaimed, "I must be dreaming!" when something great happens or when you feel too happy that this could be reality. In the dream world, anything is possible. It is a place where you can go back to those childhood times you've longed for so much, a place where you can meet anyone you want and make new experiences with them, a place where you can fly through the air or create anything you can imagine—the ideal escape, your secret haven. Imagine what a wonderful world you can create with all sorts of fun, and up until now, for however many years you have already been alive, you have never even tried it! That's what I can't believe—that most people haven't attempted to try this sooner. It's so amazing. It almost should be included in the curriculum requirement in elementary school! Everyone can benefit from learning how to lucid dream, and imagine how much happier it will make everyone become as a whole?

Well, like anything new and unfamiliar, the main thing that stops people from trying it out is because they don't know the real answer to their questions. They could even not know what questions they should be asking in the first place. People generally put off trying something if they don't know much about it. But thankfully, you are holding this book right now. Now that you have this, you can learn everything you need to know about lucid dreaming. And soon, you can say hello to a wonderful new world, just waiting to be explored and created every night when you go to bed.

What Exactly is Lucid Dreaming?
You may have heard stories from friends, heard them on television, or read a little about it on the internet. What could have prevented you from trying it out sooner could be everything you heard about being a scary and dangerous thing, how it's unnatural and should be avoided, or other misconceptions about it. But I'm here to tell you once and for all what lucid dreaming is. Lucid dreaming is simply defined as dreaming while being aware that you are in a dream. It doesn't involve calling on other forces, you don't possess other people's bodies or step into another realm, and you need any equipment or a hypnotist to do it. All you do when your lucid dream is realized, "I'm dreaming!"

. . .

What Does Lucid Dreaming Feel Like?

But of course, lucid dreaming wouldn't be so popular if it were just you sitting in a corner and telling yourself this the whole time. The power in lucid dreaming lies in the fact that everything changes once you are aware you are dreaming. You don't just let things happen to you. You can control them. When you dream, you normally believe and act as if you are in the real world. You don't question things happening even if they are bizarre, and you don't try to do impossible things because you know that it won't happen. But when you become aware that whatever place you are in is not the real world, anything can happen. You abandon all fears you have in the real world, fears caused by getting hurt, dying, getting embarrassed, or impossibility. You abandon everything holding you back in the real world because you know that nothing can hurt you in a dream. And therein lies the power.

For me, the closest thing I can use to describe it is the movie "The Matrix". Imagine a world where you are as strong as you feel when you see things happen before you that you normally wouldn't think could happen because you change the world around you with nothing but your mind and your true sense of belief that you can do it. Think of normal dreaming as being in the matrix without being told that you were not in reality. You wouldn't attempt to do extraordinary things because you would just be floating along, thinking it was not possible. But when you realize that nothing is real, just like how the characters in the film did, you can start to "bend the spoon," as the little kid said. Only, as the child said, you aren't bending the spoon. You are only bending yourself, your mind.

Who Can Lucid Dream?

There isn't a requirement for lucid dreaming, anyone can

train themselves to do it. You don't have to be a shaman or an intensely spiritual person or be gifted with psychic powers. All you need is an open mind and the proper training. This book teaches you how to do it in the next chapters.

End of Sneak Peek.

Lucid Dreaming: A Guide to Lucid Dreams That Teaches You How to Lucid Dream and Control Dreams

https://books2read.com/u/m2YJnd

©Copyright 2022 by Angel Mendez
All rights Reserved
In no way is it legal to reproduce, duplicate, or transmit any part of this document in either electronic means or in printed format. Recording of this publication is strictly prohibited and any storage of this document is not allowed unless with written permission from the publisher. All rights are reserved.
Respective authors own all copyrights not held by the publisher.

Created with Vellum

www.ingramcontent.com/pod-product-compliance
Lightning Source LLC
LaVergne TN
LVHW021736060526
838200LV00052B/3301